Kindersley at Adder

Kindersley

Emma Lloyd-Jones

To Martin &
Josephine,

Best wishes,

Emma

20 Oct 2010

see p. 6.

To David and to the flourishing Workshop
LIDA

And
To all those who have worked and are working at
Addenbrooke's for the benefit of patients
LIDA & GRAHAM

I am glad that this book so clearly shows the way in which beauty can enhance our complex hospital buildings. It is very satisfying to have been associated with the Cardozo Kindersley Workshop for so many years.

Tony Deakin, Chairman, Addenbrooke's NHS Trust

Kindersley at Addenbrooke's Hospital

ABOUT CARE FOR PEOPLE AND BEAUTY

W Graham Cannon & Lida Lopes Cardozo Kindersley

CARDOZO KINDERSLEY CAMBRIDGE 2000

Cut in marble for St. Giles' Cathedral, Edinburgh

Copyright © 2000 Lida Lopes Cardozo Kindersley and W Graham Cannon
British Library Cataloguing in Publication Data
ISBN 1 874426 12 0

Copies of this or any other Cardozo Kindersley publication are available from
The Cardozo Kindersley Workshop
152 Victoria Road, Cambridge CB4 3DZ, UK
Telephone 01223 362170

Designed by Lida Lopes Cardozo Kindersley, W Graham Cannon, Emma Lloyd-Jones and Sarah Charlesworth, using the series layout designed by Eiichi Kono.
Production by Lida Lopes Cardozo Kindersley and Emma Lloyd-Jones.
Printed by BAS Printers Limited UK
Photographs by Michael Manni Photographic, Addenbrooke's Hospital Archives and the Cardozo Kindersley Archives (throughout) and Simon Charlesworth (page 8)

The body text has been set in 12pt Emilida, a typeface designed by Lida Lopes Cardozo Kindersley, digitised by ITA Kono Design and commissioned by Timothy Guy Design for EMI.

Contents

Welsh slate, painted & gilded to mark the 175th Anniversary of The Lancet at their editorial offices in London

The History of Addenbrooke's Hospital, Cambridge

Addenbrooke's Hospital at Cambridge admitted its first patients to a building in what is now Trumpington Street, in October 1766. The founder of the Hospital, Dr John Addenbrooke, died in 1719. His wife, who enjoyed a life interest in his estate, died only a few months after her husband in 1720. In his will John Addenbrooke left his quite modest fortune to erect and maintain a hospital for the poor. The Trustees of his will were so dilatory in carrying out his instructions that the Hospital was not completed, with beds for up to 20 patients, until 47 years after his death.

Addenbrooke's Hospital in 1770

The original small building in Trumpington Street proved to be inadequate and by 1817 a committee was formed to consider the need to enlarge the Hospital. This development, which involved the demolition of much of the original building, was completed by 1825. Two wings were added and space provided for patients who, when cured, were still too weak to look after themselves.

The new frontage of Addenbrooke's Hospital in 1823

The need constantly to expand and develop has been a characteristic of hospitals for many years. By 1860 Addenbrooke's was again overcrowded and its design was thought to be old fashioned and inconvenient. The principal needs were listed as:

a)   a large waiting hall and dispensary for out-patients and three separate rooms for doctors

b)   more cubic space per bed – the recommended figure was 1600 cubic feet – improved water closets and some two or three bed wards for patients with infectious diseases

c)   enlarged kitchens so that 'the health of the servants would be more assured'

d)   speaking tubes and lifts 'to economise labour'

e)   a Porters' Lodge.

In 1862 Sir Matthew Digby Wyatt was appointed architect for this virtually new building which would provide accommodation for 100 patients. A handsome watercolour painted by Sir Matthew is on display near the entrance to the present hospital and his design remains intact, though with changes and additions not always so handsome, until the present day. When the Trumpington Street buildings were rebuilt for the University to provide the present Judge Institute for Management Studies, the front façade had to be retained. It is of historical and architectural significance, and it now exists with its original glory enhanced by colour.

The Judge Institute for
Management Studies

Addenbrooke's Hospital in 1904

The last patient was moved from the old Addenbrooke's Hospital to the new Hospital in Hills Road in October 1984. The buildings which had served the sick of Cambridge and far beyond for over 200 years were handed over to the

Nurses at Addenbrooke's Hospital in 1907

University of Cambridge. The new Hospital however had been in planning since 1958 and the first part was opened by HM the Queen on 28 May 1962.

Addenbrooke's, Hills Road in 1964

It is a far call from the Hospital as it was in 1870 to the one at Hills Road one hundred years later. By then not only had Addenbrooke's become a fully-fledged undergraduate and post-graduate teaching hospital, but also the University of Cambridge had established a Clinical School with research and teaching facilities on the same site, all in accordance with the master plan drawn up in the early 1960s.

The long main corridors act as art galleries

And still the pace of growth continues. As we enter a new
Millennium, new buildings appear on the site which are
provided by other research bodies such as the Medical
Research Council, or by pharmaceutical firms such as Smith
Kline Beecham.

Addenbrooke's Hospital from the air in 1999

Such a rate of growth brings with it its own problems and the
need to humanise and to provide visual pleasure is something
which has exercised the planners from the earliest days. It
was in this belief that in 1960 the architect of the new Hospital,
S.E.T. Cusdin approached David Kindersley for his ideas on
the lettering of internal signs. This approach began a
collaboration between the Hospital and the Kindersley
Workshop which is the subject of this book.

Art in Addenbrooke's

Although those responsible for the planning, building and running of the new Addenbrooke's Hospital were aware of the need to create a human and non-threatening environment, the pressure to provide the complex range of medical, nursing and other services quickly had prevented much being done in a systematic way.

Coney Island. Alecto print

The Addenbrooke's Art Project – as it was originally called – began in 1987 when a physician, John Stark, a surgeon, Bob Whitaker, and the former House Governor, Graham Cannon, realised the potential of the many open areas and long corridors for displaying works of art. With money from the Hospital's own trust funds, a substantial collection of Alecto prints was purchased, most of them signed limited editions.

Addenbrooke's Hospital, watercolour by David Gentleman

David Gentleman also allowed a limited edition of his watercolour of the Old Addenbrooke's Hospital to be made for sale, the profits going to the Art Fund and used mainly for framing the Alecto prints. Many of the framed reproductions are to be seen in the corridors, although they are also to be found in waiting areas and on the wards. The corridors provide an excellent opportunity to create murals and the art section of the University of the Third Age decorated two heavily used but otherwise dismal walls. The Art Director of the Hills Road Sixth Form College suggested a similar project for his advanced students and a group of these tackled a corridor 126 yards long which leads from the main concourse to the Rosie Maternity Hospital. This was, and still is, an outstanding success.

The Clowns Mural by students of the Hills Road Sixth Form College

The same College has done further work including a ceiling painting in a minor surgical operating theatre.

One of the objectives of the project was to introduce works of art by local artists. The first such could be said to be the Kindersley plaque commemorating the opening of the Hospital in 1962 and described more fully on page 28.

Under the auspices of the Art Project, and using a generous donation from a local benefactor Sir Arthur Marshall, the Hospital purchased two sets of pictures from the Cambridge Drawing Society in 1989 and 1990: most were small and particularly suitable for patients' rooms where they have been placed. The Hospital has been fortunate too in receiving donations of work from local artists. The late Professor

Denham has donated an attractive set of watercolours of rural pubs and river scenes in Suffolk and Cambridge; Mrs Burrell, widow of Anthony, has given four large paintings of his on permanent loan.

The Throw-in by Roy Calne

One of the side effects of the Project was the revelation of the number of highly professional artists on the staff. A number of them have given paintings to the Hospital. Groups of the works of the surgeon, the late David Dunn, and of the former Professor of Surgery, Sir Roy Calne FRS (to mention only two), are displayed in a corridor near to the operating theatre.

Daphne Hardy Henrion lent a most attractive terracotta sculpture.

Mother and children by Daphne Hardy Henrion

For obvious reasons of cost the introduction of sculpture has
been one of the most difficult objectives to achieve. The main
contribution so far has been the large wall mounted sculpture
'Futurian' by the eminent sculptor Michael Kenny RA.

*Futurian by
Michael Kenny*

This has transformed an otherwise enormously blank
brick wall facing the main approach to the Hospital. It was
decided that this important work by Kenny required proper
identification and the commission to David Kindersley
resulted in another work of art providing a fitting introduction
to the catalogue of Kindersley work at Addenbrooke's Hospital
which follows.

*The Kindersley
Futurian slate*

THIS STONE WAS LAID
BY
HER MAJESTY
QUEEN ELIZABETH
THE QUEEN MOTHER
HONORARY PRESIDENT
of St MARY'S HOSPITAL
ON THE
10TH OF MARCH 1983

Green slate floor plaque for St. Mary's Hospital, London

TO COMMEMORATE THE VISIT OF
HER MAJESTY QUEEN ELIZABETH THE QUEEN MOTHER
ON 9TH JUNE 1998, MARKING THE 50TH ANNIVERSARY OF
HER MAJESTY'S FIRST VISIT AS PATRONESS

Green slate plaque for Queens' College, Cambridge

David Kindersley, a pupil of Eric Gill before the Second World War, first established his Workshop at Barton, Cambridge in 1946. When David Kindersley died in 1995 his widow Lida ran the Workshop single-handed. In 1998 she married Graham Beck, who now helps with the management of the Workshop.

Cutting letters with hammer & chisel is the way we have control of the incisive moment

The Workshop has undergone changes in location, but its ethos and the enthusiasm of those who work as part of it remain unchanged. Some forty apprentices have been trained and the importance placed on learning the skills of lettercutting continues today.

At Cambridge David was introduced to the University Printer, Brooke Crutchley, beginning an association with the University of Cambridge which is still productive, as can be seen from other commissions which will be the subject of another book.

David working on scaffold at the Cambridge University Press

Here too David met Stanley Morison and John Dreyfus, both revered typographical scholars in England, and this relationship carried forward David's abiding interest in the production of typefaces and signs.

The Workshop at Chesterton in the 1970s

Whilst at Barton in 1953 came one of the biggest jobs the Kindersley Workshop had tackled – the carving of relief maps for the American War Cemetery at Madingley. The beautiful maps, inside and outside the Chapel, involved new techniques and required additional staff, but the exquisitely modelled gold and silver-plated aeroplanes, and the superb cartography are a central attraction for the thousands of visitors who come to the Cemetery every year.

Chesterton Tower, the Workshop from 1967 to 1977

David at work at Chesterton

In 1967 the Workshop moved to Chesterton. At the time of the move David was in America, lecturing and sorting out the Eric Gill archive at the William Andrews Clark Library at Los Angeles. On his return he started work on a series of decorative alphabets which, printed and hand coloured, were produced in a limited edition. A silk-screened version was later donated to Addenbrooke's Hospital by Professor and Mrs Austin Gresham and is on display in the main corridor.

Four of David's handcoloured experimental alphabets

David & Lida at the beginning of their partnership

The most significant change in the Workshop history occurred in 1976 when Lida Lopes Cardozo joined as an apprentice. From this small beginning grew a partnership, professional and personal, which lasted until David's death. Lida had already taken on the task of leading the Workshop and now heads a small and active workforce.

Another major event was the move of the Workshop in 1977 from Chesterton to its present premises at 152 Victoria Road, Cambridge. The building, which is home to Lida, Graham, and her three sons by David, used to be an infants' school. It has been described as having 'the creative, ebullient air of a Renaissance workshop' * and it is from this Workshop that most of the work described in this book was carried out.

**Montague Shaw. David Kindersley His Work and Workshop, publ. 1989 p27*

The Workshop today at Victoria Road

At work

Before describing this work, something should first be said about the importance of aesthetic excellence in public buildings – a conviction illustrated by many Kindersley works up and down the country in public places, town halls and hospitals in particular. People in hospitals, whether patients, visitors or staff, are subject to many stresses. It is no coincidence that David Kindersley was first commissioned by Addenbrooke's Hospital to design an alphabet which could be used in the production of internal signs in an attempt to reduce the bewilderment so often experienced by visitors to the complex and frightening buildings which are today's hospitals.

In a book published in 1995* the concept of beauty in buildings was described. 'Yet without the sense or reality of beauty how can we claim our buildings are complete, truly fit for human use ...?' And again ' ..."Beauty" is a missing primary ingredient, contributing to the disappointing environments that are found in so many hospitals ...'

The tools of a letter cutter

* Keith Critchlow & Jon Allen, The Whole Question of Health, publ. 1995. The Prince of Wales Institute of Architecture, pp 5 & 31.

Kindersley Work at Addenbrooke's
Signs and Lettering

David Kindersley was commissioned to design an alphabet using lower-case and upper-case lettering. This alphabet was to be used consistently for all internal and external signs and the letters were executed in black plastic inlaid into a yellow plastic background. Sadly, few, if any, of these remain today. One of the reasons for this is that titles have changed: there is for example now no such post as 'Almoner'. Another reason for their disappearance is the need for continuing and rapid change in direction signing as new buildings, new departments, new posts and titles take the place of old ones. The proposal in 1961 to unify in a style which was both clear and attractive was at the time unique; attempts are still being made to achieve the goal of unified signs.

**Clinic 6
Medical photography
Almoner
Laboratories
Administration**

An example of a sign using the alphabet David designed especially for the Hospital

Addenbrooke's was the first major teaching hospital to be completely rebuilt since the 1930s and this was no doubt a factor influencing the decision to invite the Queen to perform the opening ceremony. Another was the fact that the then Chairman of the Board of Governors, Roger H Parker was also Lord Lieutenant of Cambridgeshire. The beautiful hand carved slate has been positioned at the entrance to the Hospital's out-patient department through which thousands of patients and visitors pass each week.

The Opening Plaque is carved on Welsh slate and gilded. It measures 533mm x 883mm and was commissioned by the Board of Governors of the United Cambridge Hospitals.

Dedication Tablet of Hospital Chapel

The completion of the Chapel at the centre of the main hospital was an early part of the massive Stage Two of the building programme. The Bishop of Ely at the time, Dr Roberts, was himself a member of the Board of Governors and the Chapel is of course available for use by all denominations. The tablet is placed at the entrance to the Chapel which opens directly from the main Concourse.

> This Chapel was jointly dedicated by
> THE RIGHT REVEREND E J K ROBERTS DD
> Lord Bishop of Ely
> THE RIGHT REVEREND CHARLES A GRANT LCL MA
> Roman Catholic Bishop of Northampton
> THE REVEREND DR IRVONWY MORGAN MA BD PhD
> Moderator of the Free Church Federal Council
> 23rd November 1972

Chapel Dedication Tablet made of Welsh slate and measuring 360mm x 970mm

Personal letterhead designed by David Kindersley for the architect of the Hospital

34 Ringshall
Little Gaddesden
Nr. Berkhamsted
Hertfordshire
HP4 1ND
TELEPHONE 0442-84-3364

In common with most hospital rebuilding, economics dictate
that these major developments must be carried out in stages.
Stage Two of the new Addenbrooke's Hospital was an immense
leap forward, comprising as it did the central services for 1,200
beds on the site, laboratories, teaching accommodation and
research facilities as well as a further 400 beds and a vastly
extended Out-patient Department and Accident Unit. It was
appropriate that the opening of this stage was commemorated
by the planting of trees and that this was done by Roger
Parker who, although no longer Chairman of the Board, had
steered it through the early days of planning. The Kindersley
tablet, cut in Welsh slate, was designed in a deliberately
different style from the official opening plaque. It was
originally laid flat into a paved area of the courtyard outside
the Accident and Emergency Admissions Unit; it was later
raised to the vertical in the same area.

THESE TREES WERE PLANTED BY
MR R.H. PARKER CBE MC MA
TO COMMEMORATE THE OFFICIAL
OPENING OF A FURTHER STAGE OF
THE NEW HOSPITAL 21ST JULY 1973

*Opening Commemorative Plaque in Welsh slate carved to mark the opening of the major
phase in the building of the Hospital, it measures 460mm x 1830mm*

This centre was built in 1973 by the Addenbrooke's Hospital Recreational & Development Trust from funds raised by a public appeal. It was the idea of the Right Hon. Sir Frank Lee, GCMG. KCB. MA. who was a Vice-Chairman of The Board of Governors & Master of Corpus Christi College Cambridge & is named after him

The Descriptive Plaque donated by the major contractors for the new Hospital, Messrs Mowlem, to commemorate Sir Frank Lee. The slate measures 370mm x 1460mm.

The need for good recreational facilities for staff was recognised early by the Vice Chairman of the Board of Governors, Sir Frank Lee, formally Permanent Secretary of the Treasury. The Pemberton Trustees donated $2^1/_2$ acres to an independent Trust so that a recreation centre comprising two squash courts, a tennis court, a bar and a swimming pool could be built. Sir Frank also set up an appeal fund to achieve this. Sadly he died in 1971 before he could see his dream realised, but the funds were raised and the building opened in 1973. The cost of the Kindersley tablet was met by Messrs Mowlem, the main contractors of the new Hospital, as their tribute to Sir Frank Lee. His role as Chairman of the Frank Lee Trustees, who own the buildings and the site, has been taken on by Sir Francis Pemberton, and so successful has the Centre been that the facilities have been greatly enlarged since 1973.

Frank Lee Recreational Centre

The Nameplate for the Centre was given by Lady Kathleen Lee and her family at the same time as the tablet above. It is also in Welsh slate and measures 175mm x 1370mm.

The decision to start a Clinical School was one which was not taken easily or speedily. It was not until 1972 that the University Grants Committee (the UGC) announced the figures of pre- and post-graduate students and staff that it would be prepared to authorise. In the following year the University approved the recommendations of its Clinical School Planning Committee (see page 34) and the way was open to begin the appointment of professors to new Chairs, and of the first Dean, Dr T.M. Chalmers. In September 1976 the first students began their training on the wards of Addenbrooke's Hospital.

HRH THE PRINCESS MARGARET
COUNTESS OF SNOWDON
Inaugurated the Clinical School
of the University of Cambridge
on 28 October 1976

The Welsh slate commemorating the inauguration of the Clinical School measures 220mm x 670mm and is displayed in the entrance hall to the School.

The Opening of the Clinical School

So important was it for the University to begin taking clinical students that the first intakes were accepted into temporary teaching accommodation. It was not until 1980 that the new buildings of the Clinical School in the very centre of the site were completed and these were opened by the Duke of Edinburgh in his capacity of Chancellor of the University.

> H R H THE DUKE OF EDINBURGH
> CHANCELLOR OF THE UNIVERSITY
> Opened this building for the Clinical School
> on 21 November 1980

The Opening Plaque for the Clinical School is carved in Welsh slate and is gilded.
It measures 178mm x 673mm and is fixed in the entrance hall of the School.

Clinical School – Nameplate and University Shield

The architects for the new Clinical School, Messrs Cusdin,
Burden & Howitt, were the same as those for Addenbrooke's
Hospital, and the partner responsible, Dr S.E.T. Cusdin
commissioned other work than the plaques recorded above
from the Kindersley Workshop. Chief among these were the
nameplate and the coat of arms of the University of
Cambridge. These, executed in stainless steel, were completed
in November 1980 but have since been removed.

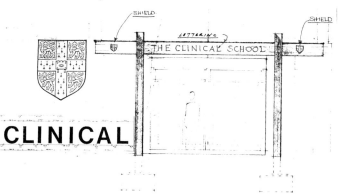

Drawing of the original nameplate and shield of the University on the canopy at the
entrance to the Clinical School

Clinical School – Commemorative Plaque

The planning of the Clinical School, its place in the national programme for recruiting and training doctors, its position in the University and its relationship with Colleges, was complex and time-consuming. In addition to 'political' issues, financial and building plans had to be drawn up and all these matters were addressed by a committee chaired by the then Master of Darwin College and Professor of Biochemistry, Sir Frank Young. To record the work of Sir Frank and his committee and the names of the Regius Professors of Physic and Clinical Deans up to 1996, a fine carved Welsh slate, coloured and gilded is in place on the stairway in the entrance hall of the Clinical School. It was completed in February 1996.

Clinical School Commemorative Plaque carved in Welsh slate, painted and gilded, together with its drawing. The plaque measures 1000mm x 320mm.

The Tom Sherwood Room

In 1996 on the retirement from the position of Clinical Dean by Professor Thomas Sherwood, it was decided to mark the occasion by naming a sitting room for clinical students after him. The carving of the nameplate above the door was completed in 1996 and carved in Welsh slate, painted and gilded.

This slate measures 610mm x 305mm

The inclusion of discrete research facilities always formed part of the planning of the Clinical School, and one such, the Centre for Protein Engineering, was opened by the then Prime Minister, Margaret Thatcher, in May 1991. The Centre was set up as an Interdisciplinary Research Centre in the University, funded by the Medical Research Council with support from industry and charitable organisations. Its purpose is to bring together in one department different disciplines and groups with overlapping interests in protein structure and design.

The Medical Research Council's Cambridge Centre for Protein Engineering Plaque, carved in Welsh slate and gilded. It measures 610mm in diameter.

The Medical Research Council (MRC), which is a body independent of the University, has from the outset of building at Hills Road had laboratories on the Addenbrooke's site. The first of these was the MRC Unit for Molecular Biology, opened in 1962, and others have since been built. Following a major benefaction from the Sackler Trust it was decided to record the Sacklers' generosity by naming the Centre after them. The plaque is placed in the main entrance to the Clinical School, to the right of the staircase.

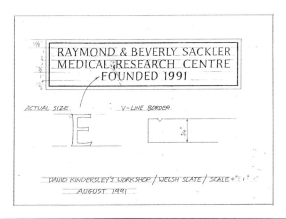

Raymond & Beverly Sackler Medical Research Centre. Plaque in Welsh slate measuring 153mm x 635mm. Letters painted off-white.

Raymond & Beverly Sackler Lecture Theatre and Meeting Lounge (currently under discussion)

The generosity of the Sacklers was once again evident when the new MRC building was built in 1998. At the time this book went to press these first designs were still being discussed and no doubt will be altered.

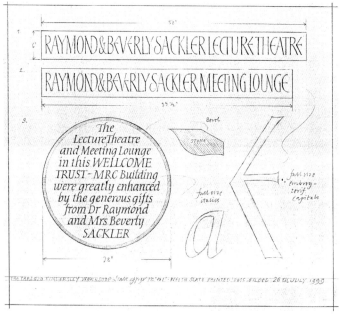

Designs submitted for new slates commemorating the further generosity of the Sackler Trust

David Evans Memorial Plaque

Dr David Evans was a consultant physician at Addenbrooke's and with Sir Roy Calne pioneered work in renal medicine. David Evans established the dialysis unit at Addenbrooke's (it was at first situated at Douglas House, a converted nursing home in Trumpington Road) and moved to Hills Road in the 1980s. David was a much loved physician and sadly died very shortly after his retirement in 1997. This memorial plaque was placed in the Unit which he founded and inspired. It is carved in Welsh slate, the lettering painted.

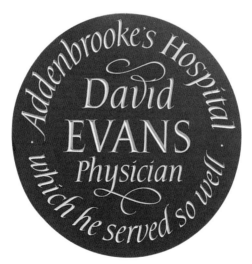

Memorial Plaque to Dr David Evans, carved in Welsh slate and measuring 450mm in diameter

Sister Harris was appointed Ward Sister to the Plastic
Surgery ward shortly after the first Cambridge-based plastic
surgeon was appointed to the Hospital in 1970. First in a small
ward at Trumpington Street, and then from 1984 in a 26-bed
unit at Hills Road, Angela Harris welded together a strong
nursing team working as colleagues with the surgeons.

> ## ⸌ANGELA HARRIS·WARD SISTER⸍
> ### She left no one untouched   1975·1997

*Memorial Plaque to Sister Angela Harris carved, painted & gilded in Welsh slate and
measuring 305mm x 1315mm*

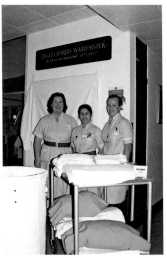

She died prematurely in her
late forties and had been
forced to stop work only
shortly before her death.
This memorial plaque,
carved in Welsh slate,
painted and gilded, was
placed in the centre of 'her'
ward, Ward D4, by the
Hospital as a tribute to her
and to her work.

Nurses on duty on Ward D4

The Departments of
Radiology & Radiotherapy
were established early in the
building of the Hospital at
Hills Road, but the need for
expensive and up to date
equipment is continuous.
John Phillips, a taxi driver by
profession, took it upon himself to raise funds to purchase
the first scanner – thus
enabling Addenbrooke's to
use the latest techniques for
diagnosing cancer. He was
so successful that further
scanners have been bought
with the funds he raised and
the Hospital decided to
honour his memory by
placing this Welsh slate,
carved, painted and gilded, at
the entrance to the
Department.

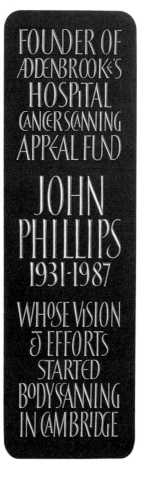

Commemorative Plaque to John Phillips, painted off-white and gilded, in the Radiology
Department of the Hospital. It measures 915mm x 280mm.

David and Lida's three boys were all born at the Rosie
Maternity Hospital, part of Addenbrooke's. From the 1960s to
the 1990s David did work for Addenbrooke's. In fact the lives of
the family with all the human activities of birth and death,
life and work, sickness and health, are intertwined with
Addenbrooke's Hospital.

*First drawing of proposed slate commemorating David Kindersley's
collaboration with Addenbrooke's over many years*

In 1995 David Kindersley died peacefully in bed at home. Five
days before this he had been told in Addenbrooke's that there
was not a lot of time left. He knew this and asked to be taken
home. It therefore seemed right to donate one piece of stone
cutting to the Hospital to inspire all and as a quiet reminder of
a man who lived in the service of beauty and a better life.

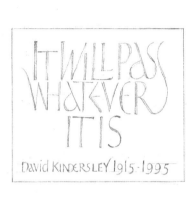

It WILL PASS
WHATEVER
IT IS

David KINDERSLEY 1915-1995

CARDOZO KINDERSLEY IN WELSH SLATE for ADDENBROOKES OCT 1996

Further sketch for David's slate. After this sketch Keith Day came to the Workshop to discuss the design which then veered towards a circle.

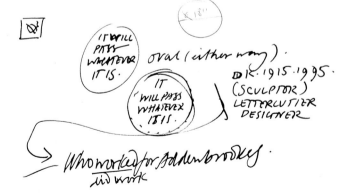

IT WILL PASS WHATEVER IT IS.

oval (either way).

IT WILL PASS WHATEVER IT IS.

DK. 1915.1995.
(SCULPTOR)
LETTERCUTTER
DESIGNER

Who worked for Addenbrookes.
did work

Lida cutting the Welsh slate circle for David's memorial in the entrance of the hospital. The finished slate is shown on the cover of this book.

The workshop has worked together with the Hospital to make the slate which is now fixed near the entrance. The quotation was one David himself drew from a Sufic source – one he was particularly fond of, one to inspire.

Postscript

To see in one small book all the years of work that this represents gives reason to contemplate. It is clear that there is a Workshop approach – or as Martin Gayford called it, 'the X ingredient' of the Kindersley Workshop.

However it is necessary to emphasise that all these stones were discussed, designed, shaped and cut by different people at varying stages of their own lives. Fashions change, in the approach both to people and things. Hospitals built today are built on different principles from those built in the 1960s. Although I would argue that lettercutting is less prone to fashion than any other activity, we do respond to the need of the moment, to people's feelings and surroundings. As they change so do we.

Legibility and decoration

As well as being a meticulous craftsman, David Kindersley was a great experimenter and was always digging deep into the question of legibility and decoration – the two extremes on the scale of letter design for form and function.

* Modern Painters Volume 4 Number 4 Winter 1991, page 51.

This is best seen in this book by looking at David's totally legible and therefore functional design for an alphabet for signs throughout the Hospital. At the time he was battling for legible motorway signs – he had designed an eccentric (by 1960s standards) capital typeface for reading fast and recognising the turn-off at high speed. Legibility was 100% but the 'fashion' of the 1950s was based on American 'clean' sans-serif lower-case; so fashion overruled function as can be seen on our motorway signs today.

David Kindersley and a motorway sign designed by him using the letterform designed for 100% legibility

We have now begun a new Millennium in which people are getting tired of the cold, clean, inhuman forms. We need warmth and a feeling of self-respect and love. Where more so than in a hospital is this so obvious?

When Graham Cannon and his colleagues began to put up paintings and pictures in Addenbrooke's Hospital they were seen as well-meaning amateurs. Nowadays Addenbrooke's, and other hospitals, have taken such activity on board as an intrinsic and important part of the administration. This is vital because it is important to make what is intrinsically a frightening place where things are done to people, into something less scary. The aim is always to make a present day hospital a welcoming place where people are comforted and helped.

To make a better life we need to be reminded of beauty and we are making small steps towards this. I hope this book will help towards these goals. It is dedicated to all those nurses, doctors and many others who together will continue to make the Hospital a worthy place of healing.

Lida Lopes Cardozo Kindersley

Acknowledgements

Illustrations on the following pages are reproduced by kind permission of:

Page 6	*Dr R.H. MacDougall*
Page 8	*The Editor, The Lancet*
Page 16	*David Gentleman*
Page 18	*Sir Roy Calne; Daphne Henrion*
Page 19	*Michael Kenny*
Page 20	*St Mary's Hospital NHS Trust;*
	The President, Queens' College Cambridge
Page 29	*Dr S.E.T. Cusdin*
Page 31	*Lady Kathleen Lee*
Page 35	*Professor Tom Sherwood*
Page 39	*Mrs Janet Evans*
Page 41	*Mrs Kathleen Phillips*

We have also been helped enormously by others in compiling these illustrations and text and would especially thank:

Keith Day – Director of Administration, Addenbrooke's NHS Trust
Philip Rundle – Addenbrooke's Hospital Archivist
Guy Noble – Addenbrooke's Art Administrator
Sally Pinnock – Secretary, University of Cambridge Clinical School
Jennifer Cornwall – Head of Administration,
*   MRC Centre, Cambridge*
Dr David McKitterick – Librarian, Trinity College, Cambridge
The Department of Medical Photography & Illustration,
*   Addenbrooke's Hospital*
Hills Road Sixth Form College